# ROASTING

# ROASTING

PETER SWANN

*p*

This is a Parragon Publishing Book

First published in 2005

Parragon Publishing
Queen Street House
4 Queen Street
Bath BA1 1HE, UK

ISBN: 1-40544-758-3

Printed in China

Produced by the Bridgewater Book Company Ltd
Photographer: Laurie Evans
Home Economist: Annie Rigg

Notes for the Reader
This book uses imperial, metric, or US cup measurements. Follow the same units of measurement throughout; do not mix imperial and metric. All spoon measurements are level: teaspoons are assumed to be 5 ml, and tablespoons are assumed to be 15 ml. Unless otherwise stated, milk is assumed to be whole, eggs and individual vegetables such as potatoes are medium, and pepper is freshly ground black pepper. Recipes using raw or very lightly cooked eggs should be avoided by infants, the elderly, pregnant women, convalescents, and anyone suffering from an illness. The times given are an approximate guide only. Preparation times differ according to the techniques used by different people and the cooking times may also vary from those given. Optional ingredients, variations, or serving suggestions have not been included in the calculations.

**Picture acknowledgments**
The Bridgewater Book Company would like to thank the following for permission to reproduce copyright material: Corbis Images, pages 6, 8, 30, 52; Getty Images, page 74.

# CONTENTS

Roasting is the technique of cooking in radiant heat and it can be used for a wide variety of ingredients, including meat, poultry, game, fish, and vegetables. All the recipes in this book have been tested in conventional ovens, so you won't have to worry about buying expensive gadgets, such as rotisseries for spit roasting, and they work just as successfully whatever fuel you are using in your kitchen.

It's unlikely you will need to rush out and buy any other extra equipment either. It's worth having a couple of good-quality, heavy roasting pans—a larger one for a turkey or a rib of beef and a smaller one in which vegetables and fish fillets can fit snugly. If the pan is too large for its contents, fat will spit messily all over the inside of the oven. If it's too small, cooking may be uneven and fat can spill over the sides, risking a dangerous fire. If the pans are heavyweight, they ensure even cooking and last a lifetime.

# INTRODUCTION

A good, flexible carving knife with a blade 12–14 inches/30–35 cm long is also essential and a knife sharpener will keep it in good condition. Always let roast meat stand, tented with foil to keep it warm, for 10–20 minutes after removing it from the oven. This evens out the residual heat and stabilizes the texture, making it easier to carve into neat slices. A carving fork is not essential, but is a worthwhile safety feature.

Meat is the most popular ingredient for roasting and, with leaner cuts now being widely available, meat roasts are even more common. However, do bear in mind that some fat is necessary to keep the meat moist during cooking and to intensify the flavor.

Lamb is the perfect choice for spring, although it is available throughout the year. Leg is ideal if you are feeding a large number of guests and rack of lamb looks attractive as well as being easy to carve. Shoulder is often said to have the sweetest meat, but it is more awkward to carve. However, you can buy it boned and rolled, if you prefer. Remember that lamb is usually served while still pink in the middle.

When oven roasting beef, larger joints are best, particularly rib. Tenderloin steak may be roasted for special occasions, but it must be well larded and basted frequently during cooking. Slightly tougher cuts, such as brisket and top

# PART ONE
# FROM THE CARVING BOARD

round, are more suitable for the slower method of pot roasting, which ensures that the meat is tender and full of flavor.

There are many different cuts of pork in a wide range of sizes that are suitable for roasting. Perhaps the most popular is boned and rolled loin, as it is very tender and easy to carve, while leg is an economical buy if you are feeding a large number of people. Unlike lamb and beef, pork must always be well cooked. Check by piercing it with a skewer to see if the juices run clear. Alternatively, use a meat thermometer. It is done when this registers 176°F/80°C.

# ROAST BEEF

**SERVES 8**

1 prime rib of beef joint, weighing 6 lb/2.7 kg

2 tsp dry English mustard

3 tbsp all-purpose flour

1 1/4 cups red wine

1 1/4 cups beef stock

2 tsp Worcestershire sauce (optional)

salt and pepper

Yorkshire pudding, to serve

Preheat the oven to 450°F/230°C.

Season the meat to taste with salt and pepper. Rub in the mustard and 1 tablespoon of the flour.

Place the meat in a roasting pan large enough to hold it comfortably and roast in the oven for 15 minutes. Reduce the temperature to 375°F/190°C and cook for 15 minutes per 1 lb/450 g, plus 15 minutes (1 3/4 hours for this joint) for rare beef or 20 minutes per 1 lb/450 g, plus 20 minutes (2 hours 20 minutes) for medium beef. Baste the meat from time to time to keep it moist, and if the pan becomes too dry, add a little stock or red wine.

Remove the meat from the oven and place on a warmed serving plate, cover with foil, and let stand in a warm place for 10–15 minutes.

To make the gravy, pour off most of the fat from the pan (reserve it for cooking the Yorkshire pudding), leaving behind the meat juices and the sediment. Place the pan on the stove over medium heat and scrape all the sediment from the bottom of the pan. Sprinkle in the remaining flour and quickly mix it into the juices with a small whisk. When you have a smooth paste, gradually add the wine and most of the stock, whisking constantly. Bring to a boil, then reduce the heat to a gentle simmer and cook for 2–3 minutes. Season with salt and pepper and add the remaining stock, if needed, and a little Worcestershire sauce, if you like.

When ready to serve, carve the meat into slices and serve on warmed plates. Pour the gravy into a warmed pitcher and take direct to the table. Serve with Yorkshire pudding.

WHEN ROASTING BEEF YOU CAN CHOOSE WHETHER YOU WANT IT TO BE WELL DONE, MEDIUM, OR RARE. YOU WILL NEED TO TIME IT CAREFULLY IF YOU WISH TO KEEP THE BEEF PINK IN THE MIDDLE. THE BEST ROAST BEEF IS A RIB COOKED ON THE BONE, BUT THIS MUST BE A GOOD SIZE.

# BEEF POT ROAST WITH POTATOES AND DILL

**SERVES 6**

2½ tbsp all-purpose flour

1 tsp salt

¼ tsp pepper

1 rolled brisket joint, weighing 3 lb 8 oz/1.6 kg

2 tbsp vegetable oil

2 tbsp butter

1 onion, finely chopped

2 celery stalks, diced

2 carrots, peeled and diced

1 tsp dill seed

1 tsp dried thyme or oregano

1½ cups red wine

⅔–1 cup beef stock

4–5 potatoes, cut into large chunks and boiled until just tender

2 tbsp chopped fresh dill, to serve

Preheat the oven to 275°F/140°C.

Mix 2 tablespoons of the flour with the salt and pepper in a shallow dish. Dip the meat to coat. Heat the oil in an ovenproof casserole and brown the meat all over. Transfer to a plate.

Add half the butter to the casserole and cook the onion, celery, carrots, dill seed, and thyme for 5 minutes. Return the meat and juices to the casserole.

Pour in the wine and enough stock to reach one-third of the way up the meat. Bring to a boil, cover, and cook in the oven for 3 hours,

turning the meat every 30 minutes. After it has been cooking for 2 hours, add the potatoes and more stock if necessary.

When ready, transfer the meat and vegetables to a warmed serving dish. Strain the cooking liquid into a pan.

Mix the remaining butter and flour to a paste. Bring the cooking liquid to a boil. Whisk in small pieces of the flour and butter paste, whisking constantly until the sauce is smooth. Pour the sauce over the meat and vegetables. Sprinkle with the fresh dill to serve.

WHEN USING A FLOUR AND BUTTER PASTE, ALSO KNOWN AS BEURRE MANIÉ, TO THICKEN A SAUCE OR GRAVY, WHISK IT INTO THE SAUCE IN SMALL PIECES, MAKING SURE EACH PIECE HAS BEEN BLENDED IN BEFORE ADDING THE NEXT.

# RACK OF LAMB

**SERVES 2**

1 trimmed rack of lamb, weighing 9–10¹/₂ oz/ 250–300 g

1 garlic clove, crushed

²/₃ cup red wine

1 fresh rosemary sprig, crushed to release the flavor

1 tbsp olive oil

²/₃ cup lamb stock

2 tbsp red currant jelly

salt and pepper

*Mint sauce*

bunch fresh mint leaves

2 tsp superfine sugar

2 tbsp water

2 tbsp white wine vinegar

Place the rack of lamb in a nonmetallic bowl and rub all over with the garlic. Pour over the wine and place the rosemary sprig on top. Cover and let marinate in the refrigerator for 3 hours or overnight if possible.

Preheat the oven to 425°F/220°C. Remove the lamb from the marinade, reserving the marinade. Pat the meat dry with paper towels and season generously with salt and pepper. Place the lamb in a small roasting pan, drizzle with the oil, and roast for 15–20 minutes, depending on whether you like your meat pink or medium. Remove the lamb from the oven and let rest, covered with foil, in a warm place for 5 minutes.

Meanwhile, pour the reserved marinade into a small pan, bring to a boil over medium heat and bubble gently for 2–3 minutes. Add the stock and red currant jelly and let simmer, stirring, until the mixture is syrupy.

To make the Mint Sauce, chop the fresh mint leaves and mix together with the sugar in a small bowl. Add the boiling water and stir to dissolve the sugar. Add the white wine vinegar and let stand for 30 minutes before serving with the lamb.

Carve the lamb into chops and serve on warmed plates with the sauce spooned over the top. Serve the Mint Sauce separately.

LAMB IS BEST IN SPRING, FROM EASTER ONWARD, WHEN IT IS AT ITS SWEETEST AND MOST SUCCULENT. ROSEMARY AND GARLIC ARE TRADITIONAL FLAVORINGS AND A GRAVY MADE WITH RED WINE AND RED CURRANT JELLY IS DIVINE. FRESH MINT FOR SAUCE IS ALSO AT ITS BEST AROUND THIS TIME. RACK OF LAMB IS AN IMPRESSIVE DISH FOR ENTERTAINING, TOO. JUST DOUBLE OR TREBLE THE INGREDIENTS, DEPENDING ON THE NUMBER OF GUESTS.

# POT ROASTED LEG OF LAMB

**SERVES 4**

1 leg of lamb, weighing
3 lb 8 oz/1.6 kg

3–4 fresh rosemary sprigs

4 oz/115 g lean
bacon slices

4 tbsp olive oil

2–3 garlic cloves, crushed

2 onions, sliced

2 carrots, sliced

2 celery stalks, sliced

1 1/4 cups dry
white wine

1 tbsp tomato paste

1 1/4 cups lamb or
chicken stock

3 medium tomatoes,
peeled, quartered, and
seeded

1 tbsp chopped
fresh parsley

1 tbsp chopped fresh
oregano or marjoram

salt and pepper

fresh rosemary sprigs,
to garnish

Wipe the lamb all over with paper towels, trim off any excess fat, and season to taste with salt and pepper, rubbing in well. Lay the sprigs of rosemary over the lamb, cover evenly with the bacon slices, and tie securely in place with kitchen string.

Heat the oil in a skillet and pan-fry the lamb over medium heat for 10 minutes, turning several times. Remove from the skillet.

Preheat the oven to 325°F/160°C. Transfer the oil from the skillet to a large ovenproof casserole and cook the garlic and onions for 3–4 minutes until the onions are starting to soften. Add the carrots and celery and cook for an additional few minutes.

Lay the lamb on top of the vegetables and press down to partly submerge. Pour the wine over the lamb, add the tomato paste, and let simmer for 3–4 minutes. Add the stock, tomatoes, and herbs and season to taste with salt and pepper. Return to a boil for an additional 3–4 minutes.

Cover the casserole tightly and cook in the oven for 2–2 1/2 hours until very tender.

Remove the lamb from the casserole and, if you like, remove the bacon and herbs together with the string. Keep the lamb warm. Strain the juices, skimming off any excess fat, and serve in a pitcher. The vegetables may be put around the joint or in a dish. Garnish with rosemary sprigs.

THIS DISH FROM THE ABRUZZI REGION OF ITALY USES A SLOW COOKING METHOD. THE MEAT ABSORBS THE FLAVORINGS AND BECOMES VERY TENDER.

# ROAST LAMB
# WITH ORZO

**SERVES 4**

1 boned leg or shoulder of lamb, weighing about 1 lb 10 oz/750 g

$^1/_2$ lemon, thinly sliced

1 tbsp chopped fresh oregano

4 large garlic cloves, 2 finely chopped and 2 thinly sliced

1 lb 12 oz/800 g canned chopped tomatoes

$^2/_3$ cup cold water

pinch of sugar

1 bay leaf

2 tbsp olive oil

$^2/_3$ cup boiling water

generous 1 cup orzo or short-grain rice

salt and pepper

Preheat the oven to 350°F/180°C.

Untie the lamb and open out. Place the lemon slices along the middle and sprinkle over half the oregano, the chopped garlic, and salt and pepper to taste. Roll up the meat and tie with string. Cut slits in the lamb and insert the garlic slices.

Weigh the meat and calculate the cooking time, allowing 25 minutes per 1 lb/450 g, plus 25 minutes.

Place the tomatoes and their can juices, cold water, remaining oregano, the sugar, and bay leaf in a large roasting pan. Place the lamb on top, drizzle over the oil, and season to taste with salt and pepper.

Roast the lamb in the oven for the calculated cooking time. Fifteen minutes before the lamb will be cooked, stir the boiling water and orzo into the tomatoes. Add a little extra water if the sauce seems too thick. Return to the oven for an additional 15 minutes, or until the lamb and orzo are tender and the tomatoes are reduced to a thick sauce.

To serve, carve the lamb into slices and serve hot with the orzo and tomato sauce.

ORZO IS A VERY SMALL FORM OF PASTA THAT LOOKS LIKE FLAT WHEAT GRAINS. IT IS USED IN SOUP AND MEAT DISHES AND SERVED AS AN ACCOMPANIMENT. IN THIS RECIPE IT IS BAKED WITH LAMB AND ABSORBS THE MEAT JUICES, GIVING IT THE MOST WONDERFUL FLAVOR. THIS IS AN IMMENSELY POPULAR DISH IN GREECE, WHERE IT IS ALSO MADE WITH KID AND BEEF.

# ROAST LAMB WITH ROSEMARY AND MARSALA

**SERVES 6**

1 leg of lamb, weighing
4 lb/1.8 kg

2 garlic cloves,
thinly sliced

2 tbsp fresh or dried
rosemary leaves

8 tbsp olive oil

2 lb/900 g potatoes, cut
into 1-inch/2.5-cm cubes

6 fresh sage
leaves, chopped

²/₃ cup Marsala

salt and pepper

Preheat the oven to 425°F/220°C.

Use a small, sharp knife to make incisions all over the lamb, opening them out slightly to make little pockets. Insert the garlic slices and about half the rosemary leaves in the pockets.

Place the lamb in a roasting pan and spoon over half the oil. Roast in the oven for 15 minutes.

Reduce the oven temperature to 350°F/180°C. Remove the lamb from the oven and season to taste with salt and pepper. Turn the lamb over, return it to the oven, and roast for an additional 1 hour.

Meanwhile, spread out the cubed potatoes in a second roasting pan, pour the remaining oil over them, and toss to coat. Sprinkle with the remaining rosemary and the sage. Place the potatoes in the oven with the lamb and roast for 40 minutes.

Remove the lamb from the oven, turn it over, and pour over the Marsala. Return it to the oven with the potatoes and cook for an additional 15 minutes. Transfer the lamb to a carving board and cover with foil. Place the roasting pan over high heat and bring the juices to a boil. Continue to boil until thickened and syrupy. Strain into a warmed sauce boat or pitcher.

Carve the lamb into slices and serve with the potatoes and sauce.

SERVING TENDER SPRING LAMB ON EASTER SUNDAY TO CELEBRATE THE END OF THE LENTEN FAST IS TRADITIONAL THROUGHOUT THE MEDITERRANEAN, NOT LEAST IN ITALY WHERE THIS DISH ORIGINATES.

# ROAST HAM

**SERVES 6**

1 boneless ham joint, weighing 3 lb/1.3 kg

2 tbsp Dijon mustard

generous ³/₈ cup raw sugar

¹/₂ tsp ground cinnamon

¹/₂ tsp ground ginger

18 whole cloves

*Cumberland sauce*

2 Seville oranges, halved

4 tbsp red currant jelly

4 tbsp port

1 tsp mustard

salt and pepper

Place the joint in a large pan, cover with cold water, and gradually bring to a boil over low heat. Cover and let simmer very gently for 1 hour. Preheat the oven to 400°F/200°C.

Remove the ham from the pan and drain. Remove the rind from the ham and discard. Score the fat into a diamond-shaped pattern with a sharp knife.

Spread the mustard over the fat. Mix the sugar and ground spices together on a plate and roll the ham in it, pressing down to coat evenly.

Stud the diamond shapes with cloves and place the joint in a roasting pan. Roast in the oven for 20 minutes until the glaze is a rich golden color.

To serve hot, cover with foil and let stand for 20 minutes before carving. If the ham is to be served cold, it can be cooked a day ahead.

To make a Cumberland Sauce, remove the zest of the oranges using a citrus zester. Place the red currant jelly, port, and mustard in a small pan and heat gently until the jelly has melted. Squeeze the juice from the oranges into the pan. Add the orange zest and season to taste with salt and pepper. Serve cold with ham. The sauce can be kept in a screw-top jar in the refrigerator for up to 2 weeks.

ROAST HAM HAS LONG BEEN A FAVORITE CHOICE FOR A ROAST LUNCH. HAM IS SALTED, EITHER BY SALT CURING OR SOAKING IN BRINE, AND SOME VARIETIES, SUCH AS YORK HAM, MAY BE SMOKED. SOME JOINTS MAY NEED TO BE SOAKED IN COLD WATER FOR 2 HOURS OR OVERNIGHT TO REDUCE THE SALTINESS (CHECK ON THE PACKAGING, TO SEE IF IT HAS BEEN PRESOAKED). THE SWEET GLAZE OF HAMS, OR THE SERVING OF A SWEET ACCOMPANIMENT SUCH AS CUMBERLAND SAUCE, IS TO COUNTERACT THE SALT.

# SLOW-ROASTED PORK

**SERVES 6**

1 piece of pork loin,
weighing 3 lb 8 oz/1.6 kg,
boned and rolled

4 garlic cloves, thinly
sliced lengthwise

1 1/2 tsp finely chopped
fennel fronds or
1/2 tsp dried fennel

4 cloves

1 1/4 cups dry white wine

1 1/4 cups water

salt and pepper

Preheat the oven to 300°F/150°C.

Use a small, sharp knife to make incisions all over the pork, opening them out slightly to make little pockets. Place the garlic slices in a small strainer and rinse under cold running water to moisten. Spread out the fennel on a saucer and roll the garlic slices in it to coat. Slide the garlic slices and the cloves into the pockets in the pork. Season the meat all over to taste with salt and pepper.

Place the pork in a large ovenproof dish or roasting pan. Pour in the wine and water. Cook in the oven, basting the meat occasionally, for 2 1/2–2 3/4 hours, or until the pork is tender but still quite moist.

If you are serving the pork hot, transfer it to a carving board, cover with foil, and let rest before cutting it into slices. If you are serving it cold, let it cool completely in the cooking juices before removing and slicing.

READY-PREPARED BONED AND ROLLED PORK LOIN IS AVAILABLE FROM SUPERMARKETS.

# ROAST PORK WITH CRACKLING

**SERVES 4**

1 piece of pork loin, weighing 2 lb 4 oz/1 kg, boned and the rind removed and reserved

2 tbsp mustard

salt and pepper

*Gravy*

1 tbsp flour

1 1/4 cups cider, apple juice, or chicken stock

*Apple sauce*

1 lb/450 g tart cooking apples

3 tbsp water

1 tbsp superfine sugar

1/2 tsp ground cinnamon (optional)

1 tbsp butter (optional)

Preheat the oven to 400°F/200°C.

Score the pork rind thoroughly with a sharp knife and sprinkle with salt. Place it on a wire rack on a baking sheet and roast in the oven for 30–40 minutes until the crackling is golden brown and crisp. This can be cooked in advance, leaving room in the oven for roast potatoes.

Season the pork well with salt and pepper and spread the fat with the mustard. Place in a roasting pan and roast in the center of the oven for 20 minutes. Reduce the oven temperature to 375°F/190°C and cook for an additional 50–60 minutes until the meat is a good color and the juices run clear when it is pierced with a skewer.

ROAST PORK CAN BE DELICIOUS OR DISAPPOINTING. IT IS ALL TO DO WITH THE QUALITY OF THE PORK AND WHETHER THE FAT WILL "CRACKLE" PROPERLY. THE CRACKLING IS ALL IMPORTANT. IT IS THE FAVORITE PART OF THE JOINT, AND UNLESS IT IS CRISP AND CRUNCHY, THE WHOLE MEAL WILL BE A DISAPPOINTMENT. THE BEST JOINTS OF PORK FOR ROASTING ARE THE LEG AND THE LOIN. CHOOSE THE LEG IF YOU ARE CATERING FOR LARGE NUMBERS, ALTHOUGH THE LOIN, WHICH CAN BE BOUGHT IN SMALLER SIZES, IS THE BEST FOR CRACKLING.

Remove the meat from the oven and place on a warmed serving plate, cover with foil, and let stand in a warm place.

To make the gravy, pour off most of the fat from the roasting pan, leaving the meat juices and the sediment. Place the pan over low heat. Sprinkle in the flour, whisking well. Cook the paste for a couple of minutes, then add the cider a little at a time until you have a smooth gravy. Boil for 2–3 minutes until it is the required consistency. Season well with salt and pepper and pour into a warmed serving pitcher.

Carve the pork into slices and serve on warmed plates with pieces of the crackling and the gravy.

To make the Apple Sauce, peel, core, and slice the cooking apples into a medium pan. Add the water and sugar, and cook over low heat for 10 minutes, stirring occasionally. A little ground cinnamon and butter can be added, if you like. Beat well until the sauce is thick and smooth— use a hand mixer for a really smooth finish. Serve the pork with the Apple Sauce.

# PORK WITH SWEET BELL PEPPERS

**SERVES 4–6**

1 piece of pork shoulder, weighing 2 lb/900 g, boned and trimmed, but left in 1 piece

1 cup dry white wine

6 garlic cloves, crushed

2 dried ancho or pasilla chilies

about 4 tbsp olive oil

2 large onions, chopped

4 red or green bell peppers, or a mixture, broiled, peeled, seeded, and sliced

1/2 tsp hot paprika

1 lb 12 oz/800 g canned chopped tomatoes

2 fresh thyme sprigs

2 fresh parsley sprigs

salt and pepper

Place the pork in a nonmetallic bowl. Pour over the wine and add 4 of the garlic cloves. Cover with plastic wrap and let marinate in the refrigerator for at least 8 hours.

Place the chilies in a heatproof bowl and pour over enough boiling water to cover. Let stand for 20 minutes to soften, then seed and chop. Set them aside.

Preheat the oven to 325°F/160°C.

Heat 4 tablespoons of oil in a large, heavy-bottom ovenproof casserole over medium-high heat. Add the onions and sauté for 3 minutes, then add the remaining garlic, chilies, bell pepper slices, and paprika and sauté for an additional 2 minutes until the onions are soft, but not brown. Use a slotted spoon to transfer the mixture to a plate, leaving as much oil as possible in the bottom of the casserole.

Drain the pork, reserving the marinade, and pat dry. Add the pork to the casserole, and cook until brown on both sides.

Return the onion mixture to the casserole with the pork and stir in the reserved marinade, tomatoes and their can juices, the herbs, and salt and pepper to taste. Bring to a boil, scraping any glazed bits from the bottom of the pan. Cover, transfer the casserole to the oven, and cook for 1 hour, or until the pork is tender. If the juices are too thin, remove the pork from the casserole and keep warm. Place the casserole over high heat and let the juices bubble until reduced.

Taste and adjust the seasoning. Cut the pork into serving pieces and serve with the bell peppers and sauce from the casserole.

COOKING "AL CHILINDRÓN" IS POPULAR THROUGHOUT SPAIN, BUT IT WAS ORIGINALLY FROM THE NORTHERN REGIONS OF NAVARRE AND ARAGON, WHERE THE RUGGED CONDITIONS DEMANDED HEARTY, FULL-FLAVORED DISHES. THE DRIED CHILIES IN THIS RECIPE PROVIDE A CLOSE-TO-AUTHENTIC FIERY FLAVOR, SO FOR A MILDER DISH, USE DRIED ÑORA CHILIES. YOU NEED TO MARINATE THE PORK FOR AT LEAST 8 HOURS, PREFERABLY OVERNIGHT.

It is hard to believe that a couple of generations ago, roast chicken was a rare and expensive treat reserved for special occasions. Modern farming methods have made it much less costly and more routine, often at the expense of both flavor and texture. However, good-quality, free-range chicken still has that special magic and remains a family favorite. Squab chickens, also known as poussin, are popular and fun to serve, each bird providing a single portion.

Turkey has been the first choice for feeding large gatherings for a long time and that festive favorite, goose, while rather expensive, has made a great comeback in recent years in Europe. Duckling, too, has become very fashionable, having moved on from its bistro guise in sticky orange sauce. It's certainly worth trying the clever boned and stuffed recipe in this chapter, which provides a delicious and surprisingly substantial feast.

# PART TWO
# THE GAMEKEEPER'S CHOICE

All kinds of game are now much more widely available, as venison and feathered game are increasingly farmed. Fresh game remains a seasonal treat, but it is often available frozen all year round. Like poultry, frozen game should be thoroughly thawed before cooking. These days, most game is sold oven-ready, so you don't have to endure the time-consuming, tricky, and messy tasks of plucking and drawing it yourself.

Roast pheasant, guinea fowl, or a saddle of venison still retain an air of being extra special, so they are ideal for dinner parties. Quail are also an excellent choice as they cook very quickly, taste wonderful, and are much meatier than their size would suggest.

# ROAST CHICKEN

**SERVES 6**

1 free-range chicken, weighing 5 lb/2.25 kg

2 oz/55 g butter

2 tbsp chopped fresh lemon thyme

1 lemon, quartered

1/2 cup white wine

salt and pepper

6 fresh thyme sprigs, to garnish

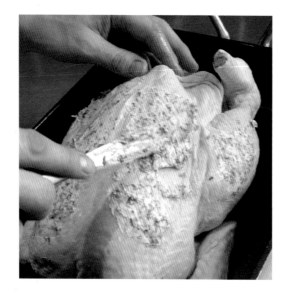

Preheat the oven to 425°F/220°C. Make sure the chicken is clean, wiping it inside and out using paper towels, and place in a roasting pan.

Place the butter in a bowl and soften with a fork, then mix in the thyme and season well with salt and pepper. Butter the chicken all over with the herb butter, inside and out, and place the lemon quarters inside the body cavity. Pour the wine over the chicken.

Roast the chicken in the center of the oven for 20 minutes. Reduce the temperature to 375°F/190°C and continue to roast for an additional 1 1/4 hours, basting frequently. Cover with foil if the skin starts to brown too much. If the pan dries out, add a little more wine or water.

Test that the chicken is cooked by piercing the thickest part of the leg with a sharp knife or skewer and making sure the juices run clear. Remove from the oven.

Remove the chicken from the roasting pan and place on a warmed serving plate to rest, covered with foil, for 10 minutes before carving.

Place the roasting pan on the top of the stove and bubble the pan juices gently over low heat until they have reduced and are thick and glossy. Season to taste with salt and pepper.

Serve the chicken with the pan juices and sprinkle with the thyme sprigs.

SIMPLY ROASTED, WITH LOTS OF THYME AND LEMON, CHICKEN PRODUCES A SUCCULENT GASTRONOMIC FEAST FOR MANY OCCASIONS. TRY TO BUY A GOOD FRESH CHICKEN AS FROZEN BIRDS DO NOT HAVE AS MUCH FLAVOR. YOU CAN STUFF YOUR CHICKEN WITH A TRADITIONAL DRESSING, SUCH AS SAGE AND ONION, OR FRUIT LIKE APRICOTS AND PRUNES, BUT OFTEN THE BEST WAY IS TO KEEP IT SIMPLE.

# SQUAB CHICKENS WITH HERBS AND WINE

**SERVES 4**

5 tbsp fresh brown
bread crumbs

7/8 cup lowfat
mascarpone cheese

5 tbsp chopped
fresh parsley

5 tbsp snipped
fresh chives

4 squab chickens

1 tbsp corn oil

1 lb 8 oz/675 g young
spring vegetables, such as
carrots, zucchini, sugar
snap peas, baby corn,
and turnips, cut into
small chunks

1/2 cup boiling
chicken stock

2 tsp cornstarch

2/3 cup dry white wine

salt and pepper

Preheat the oven to 425°F/220°C.

Mix the bread crumbs, one-third of the mascarpone, and 2 tablespoons each of the parsley and chives together in a bowl. Season well with salt and pepper. Spoon into the neck ends of the squab chickens. Place on a rack in a roasting pan, brush with oil, and season well.

Roast in the oven for 30–35 minutes, or until the juices run clear when the thickest part of the meat is pierced with a skewer.

Place the vegetables in a shallow ovenproof dish in a single layer and add half the remaining herbs with the stock.

Cover and bake in the oven for 25–30 minutes until tender. Lift the squab chickens onto a warmed serving plate and skim any fat from the juices in the pan. Add the vegetable juices and place the pan over medium heat.

Blend the cornstarch with the wine and whisk into the sauce with the remaining mascarpone. Whisk until boiling, then add the remaining herbs. Season to taste with salt and pepper. Spoon the sauce over the squab chickens and serve with the vegetables.

Squab chickens are simple to prepare, quick to cook, and can be easily cut in half lengthwise with a sharp knife.

# YULETIDE GOOSE WITH HONEY AND PEARS

**SERVES 4**

1 oven-ready goose,
weighing 7 lb 12 oz–
10 lb/3.5–4.5 kg

1 tsp salt

4 pears

1 tbsp lemon juice

2 oz/55 g butter

2 tbsp honey

lemon slices, to garnish

seasonal vegetables,
to serve

Preheat the oven to 425°F/220°C.

Rinse the goose and pat dry. Use a fork to prick the skin all over, then rub with the salt. Place the bird upside down on a rack in a roasting pan. Roast in the oven for 30 minutes. Drain off the fat. Turn the bird over and roast for 15 minutes. Drain off the fat. Reduce the temperature to 350°F/180°C and roast for 15 minutes per 1 lb/450 g. Cover with foil 15 minutes before the end of the cooking time. Check that the bird is cooked by inserting a knife between the legs and body. If the juices run clear, it is cooked. Remove from the oven.

Peel and halve the pears and brush with lemon juice. Melt the butter and honey in a pan over low heat, then add the pears. Cook, stirring, for 5–10 minutes until tender. Remove from the heat, arrange the pears around the goose, and pour the sweet juices over the bird. Garnish with lemon slices and serve with seasonal vegetables.

GOOSE FAT IS SIMPLY PERFECT FOR ROASTING (AND SAUTÉEING) POTATOES, SO DON'T WASTE IT. POUR ANY THAT YOU ARE NOT ABOUT TO USE IMMEDIATELY INTO A JAR WITH A SCREW TOP AND STORE IN THE REFRIGERATOR.

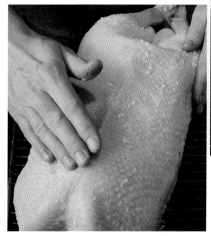

# BONED AND STUFFED ROAST DUCKLING

**SERVES 6–8**

1 duckling, weighing
4 lb/1.8 kg (dressed
weight); boned with wings
cut off at the first joint

1 lb/450 g flavored
bulk sausage

1 small onion,
finely chopped

1 eating apple, cored and
finely chopped

1/2 cup no-soak dried
apricots, finely chopped

1/2 cup chopped walnuts

2 tbsp chopped
fresh parsley

1 large or 2 smaller duck
breasts, skin removed

salt and pepper

*Apricot sauce*

14 oz/400 g canned
apricot halves

2/3 cup stock

1/2 cup Marsala

1/2 tsp ground cinnamon

1/2 tsp ground ginger

salt and pepper

Wipe the duckling with paper towels both inside and out. Lay it skin-side down on a board and season well with salt and pepper.

Mix the bulk sausage, onion, apple, apricots, walnuts, and parsley together. Season well with salt and pepper. Form into a large sausage shape.

Lay the duck breast(s) on the whole duckling and cover with the dressing. Wrap the whole duckling around the dressing and carefully tuck in any leg and neck flaps.

Preheat the oven to 375°F/190°C.

Sew the duckling up the back and across both ends with fine string. Try to use one piece of string so that you can remove it in one go. Mold the duckling into a good shape and place, sewn-side down, on a wire rack over a roasting pan.

Roast in the oven for 1 1/2–2 hours, basting occasionally. Pour off some of the fat in the pan. When it is cooked, the duckling should be golden brown and the skin crisp.

Meanwhile, purée the apricots with syrup in a blender or food processor. Pour into a pan, add the stock, Marsala, cinnamon, and ginger and season with salt and pepper. Stir over low heat, then let simmer for 2–3 minutes.

Carve the duckling into thick slices at the table and serve with the warm Apricot Sauce.

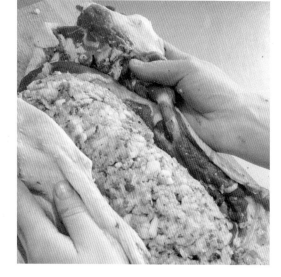

DUCKLING IS WONDERFUL TO SERVE ON A SPECIAL OCCASION, THE ONLY DRAWBACK BEING THAT THERE IS NOT MUCH MEAT ON THE BIRD AND IT CAN BE DIFFICULT TO CARVE. WHY NOT HAVE YOUR DUCKLING BONED AND THEN FILL IT WITH GOOD-QUALITY BULK SAUSAGE? IF YOU ADD A COUPLE OF DUCK BREASTS, YOU CAN MAKE A VERY SUBSTANTIAL DISH FOR 6–8 PEOPLE THAT IS EASY TO CARVE AND LOOKS WONDERFUL. SERVE WITH A SWEET SAUCE—ORANGE IS CLASSIC, BUT ONE MADE WITH CANNED APRICOTS, SPICED WITH CINNAMON, AND GINGER, IS MORE UNUSUAL.

# TRADITIONAL ROAST TURKEY
## WITH WINE AND MUSHROOMS

**SERVES 4**

1 oven-ready turkey,
weighing 11 lb/5 kg

1 garlic clove,
finely chopped

generous ⅓ cup red wine

2½ oz/75 g butter

*Dressing*

3½ oz/100 g white
mushrooms

1 onion, chopped

1 garlic clove, chopped

3 oz/85 g butter

1¾ cups fresh
bread crumbs

2 tbsp finely chopped
fresh sage

1 tbsp lemon juice

salt and pepper

*Port and cranberry sauce*

½ cup sugar

generous 1 cup port

1½ cups fresh cranberries

Preheat the oven to 400°F/200°C.

To make the dressing, clean and chop the mushrooms, place them in a pan with the onion, garlic, and butter, and cook for 3 minutes.

Remove from the heat and stir in the remaining dressing ingredients. Rinse the turkey and pat dry with paper towels. Fill the neck end with dressing and truss with string.

Place the turkey in a roasting pan. Rub the garlic over the bird and pour the wine over. Add the butter and roast in the oven for 30 minutes. Baste, then reduce the temperature to 350°F/180°C and roast for an additional 40 minutes. Baste again and cover with foil. Roast for an additional 2 hours, basting regularly. Check that the bird is cooked by inserting a knife between the legs and body. If the juices run clear, it is cooked. Remove from the oven, cover with foil, and let stand for 25 minutes.

Meanwhile, place the sugar, port, and cranberries in a pan. Heat over medium heat until almost boiling. Reduce the heat, let simmer for 15 minutes, stirring, then remove from the heat. Serve the turkey with the sauce.

MOST TURKEYS ON SALE ARE WHITE-FEATHERED VARIETIES. HOWEVER, THE DARK-FEATHERED BIRDS, KNOWN AS HERITAGE TURKEYS, ARE BECOMING INCREASINGLY POPULAR. THE SKIN MAY SHOW THE REMAINS OF DARK STUBBLE, WHICH LOOKS LESS ATTRACTIVE, BUT THE FLAVOR OF HERITAGE BIRDS IS USUALLY SUPERIOR. THE AMERICAN BRONZE, JERSEY BUFF, BOURBON RED, AND NARRAGANSETT ARE ALL FLAVORSOME, PLUMP-BREASTED BREEDS.

# ROAST TURKEY
# WITH CIDER SAUCE

**SERVES 8**

1 boneless turkey breast roast, weighing 2 lb 4 oz/ 1 kg

1 tbsp corn oil

salt and pepper

*Dressing*

2 tbsp butter

2 shallots, finely chopped

1 celery stalk, finely chopped

1 cooking apple, peeled, cored, and diced

5/8 cup prunes, pitted and chopped

generous 1/3 cup raisins

3 tbsp chicken stock

4 tbsp hard cider

1 tbsp chopped fresh parsley

*Cider sauce*

1 shallot, very finely chopped

1 1/4 cups hard cider

1/2 cup chicken stock

1 tsp cider vinegar

Preheat the oven to 375°F/190°C.

To make the dressing, melt the butter in a pan. Add the shallots and cook, stirring occasionally, for 5 minutes. Add the celery and apple and cook for 5 minutes. Add the remaining dressing ingredients, cover, and let simmer gently for 5 minutes, or until all the liquid has been absorbed. Transfer to a bowl and let cool.

Place the turkey roast on a cutting board and slice almost completely through, from the thin side toward the thicker side. Open out, place between 2 sheets of plastic wrap, and flatten with a meat mallet or rolling pin to an even thickness. Season to taste with salt. Spoon on

the cooled dressing, roll the roast around it, and tie with kitchen string. Heat the oil in a roasting pan over medium heat, add the roast, and brown all over. Transfer to the oven and roast for 1 hour 10 minutes, or until cooked through and the juices run clear when the meat is pierced with a skewer. Remove the roast from the pan and cover with foil.

To make the sauce, pour off any fat from the pan and set over medium heat. Add the shallot and half the cider and cook for 1–2 minutes, scraping any sediment from the bottom of the pan. Add the remaining cider, stock, and vinegar and cook for 10 minutes, or until reduced and thickened. Remove and discard the string from the turkey and cut into slices. Serve with the Cider Sauce.

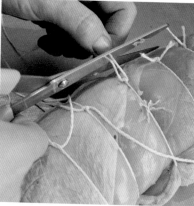

MOST SUPERMARKETS SELL BONELESS TURKEY BREAST ROAST. THERE IS NO WASTE, SO IT IS AN ECONOMICAL CHOICE WHEN ENTERTAINING AND IT FITS INTO THE OVEN MORE EASILY THAN A WHOLE BIRD. ROLLING THE TURKEY AROUND THE DRESSING HELPS TO KEEP THE MEAT MOIST DURING COOKING.

# ROAST PHEASANT
# WITH RED WINE AND HERBS

**SERVES 4**

3 1/2 oz/100 g butter,
slightly softened

1 tbsp chopped
fresh thyme

1 tbsp chopped
fresh parsley

2 oven-ready young
pheasants

4 tbsp vegetable oil

1/2 cup red wine

salt and pepper

*To serve*

honey-glazed parsnips

sautéed potatoes

freshly cooked
Brussels sprouts

Preheat the oven to 375°F/190°C.

Place the butter in a small bowl and mix in the chopped herbs. Lift the skins off the pheasants, taking care not to tear them, and push the herb butter under the skins. Season to taste with salt and pepper. Pour the oil into a roasting pan, add the pheasants, and cook in the oven for 45 minutes, basting occasionally.

Remove from the oven, pour over the wine, then return to the oven and cook for an additional 15 minutes, or until cooked through. Check that each bird is cooked by inserting a knife between the legs and body. If the juices run clear, they are cooked.

Remove the pheasants from the oven, cover with foil, and let stand for 15 minutes. Divide between individual serving plates, and serve with honey-glazed parsnips, sautéed potatoes, and freshly cooked Brussels sprouts.

ONLY YOUNG BIRDS ARE SUITABLE FOR ROASTING, AS OLDER PHEASANTS ARE FAIRLY TOUGH AND NEED A SLOWER COOKING METHOD. EVEN SO, THE MEAT ON THE LEGS TENDS TO BE QUITE TOUGH AND SINEWY, WHEREAS THE LIGHTER BREASTS ARE MORE DELICATE AND TENDER. IT IS QUITE USUAL TO SERVE ONLY THE BREASTS. KEEP THE LEG MEAT FOR MAKING A GROUND PASTA SAUCE OR USING IN A PIE. YOU CAN ALSO MAKE DELICIOUS STOCK WITH THE CARCASSES.

# GUINEA FOWL WITH CABBAGE

**SERVES 4**

1 oven-ready guinea fowl, weighing 2 lb 12 oz/1.25 kg

1/2 tbsp corn oil

1/2 apple, peeled, cored, and chopped

several fresh flat-leaf parsley sprigs, stems bruised

1 large savoy cabbage, coarse outer leaves removed, cored, and quartered

1 thick piece of smoked belly of pork, weighing about 5 oz/140 g, rind removed and cut into thin lardons, or 5 oz/140 g unsmoked lardons

1 onion, sliced

1 bouquet garni

1 1/2 tbsp chopped fresh flat-leaf parsley

salt and pepper

Preheat the oven to 475°F/240°C.

Rub the guinea fowl with the oil and season to taste inside and out with salt and pepper. Add the apple and parsley sprigs to the guinea fowl's cavity and truss to tie the legs together. Place the guinea fowl in a roasting pan and roast in the oven for 20 minutes to color the breasts. When the guinea fowl is golden brown, reduce the oven temperature to 325°F/160°C.

Meanwhile, bring a large pan of salted water to a boil. Add the cabbage and blanch for 3 minutes. Drain, rinse in cold water, and pat dry.

Place the lardons in an ovenproof casserole over medium-high heat and sauté until they give off their fat. Use a slotted spoon to remove the lardons from the casserole and set aside.

Add the onion to the fat left in the casserole and cook, stirring frequently, for 5 minutes, or until the onion is tender, but not brown. Stir the bouquet garni into the casserole with a very little salt and a pinch of pepper, then return the lardons to the casserole.

Remove the guinea fowl from the oven. Add the cabbage to the casserole, top with the guinea fowl, and cover the surface with a piece of wet waxed paper. Cover the casserole and place it in the oven for 45 minutes–1 hour, or until the guinea fowl is tender and the juices run clear when a skewer is inserted into the thickest part of the meat.

Remove the guinea fowl from the casserole and cut into serving portions. Stir the parsley into the cabbage and onion, then taste and adjust the seasoning if necessary. Serve the guinea fowl portions on a bed of cabbage and onion.

IT IS IMPORTANT NOT TO ADD TOO MUCH SALT TO THE ONION AS THE LARDONS WILL BE SALTY.

# QUAIL WITH GRAPES

**SERVES 4**

4 tbsp olive oil

8 oven-ready quail

10 oz/280 g green
seedless grapes

1 cup grape juice

2 cloves

about ⅔ cup water

2 tbsp brandy

salt and pepper

*Potato pancake*

1 lb 5 oz/600 g unpeeled
potatoes

1¼ oz/35 g unsalted
butter or pork fat

1¼ tbsp olive oil

Preheat the oven to 450°F/230°C. Parboil the potatoes for the pancake in a large pan of lightly salted water for 10 minutes. Drain and let cool completely, then peel, coarsely grate, and season to taste with salt and pepper. Set aside.

Heat the oil in a heavy-bottom skillet or ovenproof casserole large enough to hold the quail in a single layer over medium heat. Add the quail and cook on all sides until golden brown.

Add the grapes, grape juice, cloves, enough water to come halfway up the sides of the quail, and salt and pepper to taste. Cover and let simmer for 20 minutes. Transfer the quail and all the juices to a roasting pan and sprinkle with the brandy. Place in the oven and roast, uncovered, for 10 minutes.

Meanwhile, to make the Potato Pancake, melt the butter with the oil in a 12-inch/30-cm nonstick skillet over high heat. When the fat is hot, add the potatoes and spread into an even layer. Reduce the heat and cook gently for 10 minutes. Place a plate over the skillet and, wearing oven mitts, invert them so that the Potato Pancake drops onto the plate. Slide the potato back into the skillet and continue cooking for 10 minutes, or until cooked through and crisp. Slide out of the skillet and cut into 4 wedges. Keep warm until the quail are ready.

Place a Potato Pancake wedge and 2 quail on each plate. Taste the grape sauce and adjust the seasoning if necessary. Spoon the sauce over the quail and serve.

FARMED QUAIL, WEIGHING 4–5 OZ/115–140 G, ARE WIDELY AVAILABLE ALL YEAR ROUND. THEY MAY BE FRESH OR FROZEN AND ARE USUALLY OVEN-READY.

# ROAST VENISON WITH BRANDY SAUCE

**SERVES 4**

6 tbsp vegetable oil

3 lb 12 oz/1.7 kg saddle of fresh venison, trimmed

salt and pepper

fresh thyme sprigs, to garnish

freshly cooked vegetables, to serve

*Brandy sauce*

1 tbsp all-purpose flour

4 tbsp vegetable stock

3/4 cup brandy

generous 1/3 cup heavy cream

Preheat the oven to 350°F/180°C.

Heat half the oil in a skillet over high heat. Season the venison to taste with salt and pepper, add to the skillet, and cook until lightly browned all over. Pour the remaining oil into a roasting pan. Add the venison, cover with foil, and roast in the oven, basting occasionally, for 1 1/2 hours, or until cooked through. Remove

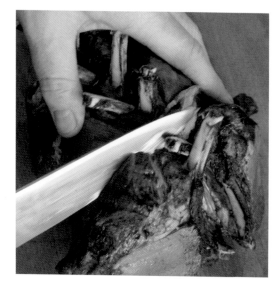

from the oven and transfer to a warmed serving platter. Cover with foil and set aside.

To make the sauce, stir the flour into the roasting pan over the stove and cook for 1 minute. Pour in the stock and heat, stirring to loosen the sediment from the bottom. Gradually stir in the brandy and bring to a boil, then reduce the heat and simmer, stirring, for 10–15 minutes until the sauce has thickened a little. Remove from the heat and stir in the cream.

Garnish the venison with thyme and serve with the Brandy Sauce and a selection of freshly cooked vegetables.

BOTH WILD AND FARMED VENISON—DEER MEAT—ARE AVAILABLE AND SURPRISINGLY INEXPENSIVE COMPARED WITH LAMB OR BEEF. IT MAY BE FRESH OR FROZEN. IT HAS A DELICATE TEXTURE AND IS HIGH IN PROTEIN, BUT LOW IN FAT, SO IT IS VERY NUTRITIOUS.

We tend to think of roasting fish as a fairly modern technique, yet even Mrs Beeton in her famous 19th-century enquire-within on household management includes recipes for roasting salmon, sole, and mackerel, although she tends to call the process baking. This signposts the differences between roasting meat or poultry and roasting fish. Firstly, fish cooks very much more rapidly than most meat and, secondly, its flesh is generally quite delicate and can easily be dried out by the high heat of the oven. Therefore, many recipes include extra ingredients, such as lemon or lime juice, wine, vegetables, bread crumbs, and herbs, as well as oil or butter, to protect it and keep it moist. These may be used as dressings, crusts, or sauces, or as a mixture of these.

You need to pay attention to the roasting times and to keep an eye on the fish while it is cooking, but roasting fish is not a difficult art and

# PART THREE
# THE OCEAN SELECTION

the results are simply mouthwatering. The crisp golden skin enclosing the succulent flesh of a well-roasted whole fish makes sea bass or porgy a spectacular dinner party dish, while fillets of all kinds, whether oily or white fish, are easy to handle and serve. In particular, meaty fish with firm flesh respond well to roasting—angler fish perhaps being the best of all, although tuna runs a close second. The texture of angler fish and even its flavor have been compared—favorably—to that of roast lamb. Seafood, such as shrimp, acquires a special flavor when roasted, with the added advantage that it takes hardly any time to cook, and there is no need to stand over it and stir.

# ROASTED SEA BASS

**SERVES 4**

1 whole sea bass, about
3–4 lb/1.3–1.8 kg, cleaned

1 small onion,
finely chopped

2 garlic cloves,
finely chopped

2 tbsp finely chopped
fresh herbs, such
as parsley, chervil,
and tarragon

1 oz/25 g anchovy fillets,
finely chopped

2 tbsp butter

²/₃ cup white wine

2 tbsp sour cream

salt and pepper

Preheat the oven to 400°F/200°C.

Remove any scales from the fish and rinse it thoroughly both inside and out. If you like, trim off the fins with a pair of scissors. Using a sharp knife, make five or six cuts diagonally into the flesh of the fish on both sides. Season well with salt and pepper, both inside and out.

Mix the onion, garlic, herbs, and anchovies together in a bowl.

Stuff the fish with half the mixture and spoon the remainder into a roasting pan. Place the sea bass on top.

Spread the butter over the fish, pour over the wine, and place in the oven. Roast for 30–35 minutes until the fish is cooked through and the flesh flakes easily.

Using a spatula, carefully remove the sea bass from the pan to a warmed serving platter. Place the roasting pan over medium heat and stir the onion mixture and juices together. Add the sour cream, mix well, and pour into a warmed serving bowl.

Serve the sea bass whole and divide at the table. Spoon a little sauce on the side.

YOU CAN USE EITHER SMALL INDIVIDUAL FISH TO SERVE AS SINGLE PORTIONS OR ONE LARGE ONE TO SHARE AMONG FAMILY OR FRIENDS. INDIVIDUAL FISH, WEIGHING 10–12 OZ/280–350 G EACH, WILL TAKE ONLY 15–20 MINUTES TO ROAST. ROUND FISH LIKE SEA BASS, PORGY, RED SNAPPER, TROUT, AND MACKEREL ARE PARTICULARLY GOOD FOR ROASTING BECAUSE THEIR SKIN CRISPS UP WELL WHILE THE FLESH STAYS DELICIOUSLY MOIST AND CREAMY. MAKE SURE YOU USE REALLY FRESH FISH IF YOU WANT THIS DISH TO SPARKLE.

# ROASTED SALMON WITH LEMON AND HERBS

**SERVES 4**

6 tbsp extra virgin
olive oil

1 onion, sliced

1 leek, sliced

juice of 1/2 lemon

2 tbsp chopped
fresh parsley

2 tbsp chopped fresh dill

1 lb 2 oz/500 g
salmon fillets

salt and pepper

freshly cooked baby
spinach leaves, to serve

*To garnish*

lemon slices

fresh dill sprigs

Preheat the oven to 400°F/200°C.

Heat 1 tablespoon of the oil in a skillet over medium heat. Add the onion and leek and cook, stirring occasionally, for 4 minutes, or until slightly softened.

Meanwhile, place the remaining oil in a small bowl with the lemon juice and herbs and season to taste with salt and pepper. Stir together well. Rinse the fish under cold running water, then pat dry with paper towels. Arrange the fish in a shallow ovenproof dish.

Remove the skillet from the heat and spread the onion and leek over the fish. Pour the oil mixture over the top, making sure that everything is well coated. Roast in the center of the preheated oven for 10 minutes, or until the fish is cooked through.

Arrange the cooked spinach on serving plates. Remove the fish and vegetables from the oven and arrange on top of the spinach. Garnish with lemon slices and sprigs of dill. Serve at once.

ALTHOUGH SALMON IS AN OILY FISH, IT HAS VERY DELICATE FLESH THAT CAN DRY OUT EASILY. THEREFORE, IT IS IMPORTANT TO MAKE SURE THAT ALL THE FILLETS ARE WELL COATED WITH THE OIL AND LEMON JUICE MIXTURE TO PROTECT THEM. KEEP AN EYE ON THE FISH DURING ROASTING TO PREVENT OVERCOOKING.

# ROASTED TUNA WITH ORANGE AND ANCHOVIES

**SERVES 4–6**

scant 1 cup freshly
squeezed orange juice

3 tbsp extra virgin
olive oil

2 oz/55 g anchovy fillets in
oil, coarsely chopped, with
the oil reserved

small pinch of dried red
pepper flakes, or to taste

1 tuna fillet, about
1 lb 5 oz/600 g

pepper

Combine the orange juice, 2 tablespoons of the olive oil, the anchovies and their oil, and red pepper flakes in a nonmetallic bowl large enough to hold the tuna and add pepper to taste. Add the tuna and spoon the marinade over it. Cover with plastic wrap and let chill in the refrigerator for at least 2 hours to marinate, turning the tuna occasionally. Remove the bowl from the refrigerator about 20 minutes before cooking to return the fish to room temperature.

Meanwhile, preheat the oven to 425°F/220°C.

Remove the tuna from the marinade, reserving the marinade, and wipe dry. Heat the remaining oil in a large skillet over high heat. Add the tuna and sear for 1 minute on each side until lightly browned and crisp. Place in a small roasting pan. Cover the pan tightly with foil.

Roast in the oven for 8 minutes for medium-rare and 10 minutes for medium-well done. Remove from the oven and set aside to rest for at least 2 minutes before slicing.

Meanwhile, place the marinade in a small pan over high heat and bring to a rolling boil. Boil for at least 2 minutes.

Transfer the tuna to a serving platter and carve into thick slices, which will probably break into chunks as you cut them. Serve the sauce separately for spooning over. The tuna can be served hot or at room temperature, but the sauce is best hot.

JUST LIKE BEEF, ROASTED TUNA CONTINUES TO COOK AFTER IT COMES OUT OF THE OVEN WHILE IT RESTS. AN EASY WAY TO CHECK WHETHER THE TUNA IS COOKED IS TO INSERT A MEAT THERMOMETER INTO IT, THROUGH THE FOIL, JUST BEFORE YOU PLACE THE COVERED PAN IN THE OVEN. WHEN THE TEMPERATURE READS 140°F/60°C, THE TUNA WILL BE MEDIUM.

# ROASTED SEAFOOD

**SERVES 4**

1 lb 5 oz/600 g new potatoes

3 red onions, cut into wedges

2 zucchini, cut into chunks

8 garlic cloves, peeled but left whole

2 lemons, cut into wedges

4 fresh rosemary sprigs

4 tbsp olive oil

12 oz/350 g unshelled raw shrimp

2 small raw squid, cut into rings

4 tomatoes, quartered

Preheat the oven to 400°F/200°C.

Scrub the potatoes to remove any dirt. Cut any large potatoes in half. Parboil the potatoes in a pan of boiling water for 10–15 minutes. Place the potatoes in a large roasting pan

together with the onions, zucchini, garlic, lemons, and rosemary sprigs.

Pour over the oil and toss to coat all the vegetables in it. Roast in the oven for 30 minutes, turning occasionally, until the potatoes are tender.

Once the potatoes are tender, add the shrimp, squid, and tomatoes, tossing to coat them in the oil, and roast for 10 minutes. All the vegetables should be cooked through and slightly charred for full flavor.

Transfer the roasted seafood and vegetables to warmed serving plates and serve hot.

MOST VEGETABLES ARE SUITABLE FOR ROASTING IN THE OVEN. TRY ADDING 1 LB/450 G PUMPKIN, SQUASH, OR EGGPLANT, IF YOU LIKE.

# ROAST ANGLER FISH WITH ROMESCO SAUCE

**SERVES 4–6**

1 angler fish tail, about
2 lb/900 g, membrane
removed

2–3 slices serrano ham

olive oil, for brushing

salt and pepper

*Romesco sauce*

1 red bell pepper, halved
and seeded

4 garlic cloves, unpeeled

2 tomatoes, halved

1/2 cup olive oil

1 slice white bread, diced

4 tbsp blanched almonds

1 fresh red chili, seeded
and chopped

2 shallots, chopped

1 tsp paprika

2 tbsp red wine vinegar

2 tsp sugar

1 tbsp water

Preheat the oven to 425°F/
220°C.

For the sauce, place the bell
pepper, garlic, and tomatoes in a
roasting pan and toss with
1 tablespoon of the oil. Roast in
the oven for 20–25 minutes, then
remove from the oven, cover with
a dish towel, and set aside for
10 minutes. Peel off the skins
and place the vegetables in a
food processor.

Heat 1 tablespoon of the
remaining oil in a skillet. Add the
bread cubes and almonds and
cook over low heat, stirring
frequently, until golden. Remove with a slotted
spoon and drain on paper towels. Add the chili,
shallots, and paprika to the skillet and cook,
stirring occasionally, for 5 minutes.

Transfer the bread and chili mixtures to the
food processor, add the vinegar, sugar, and
water, and process to a paste. With the motor
running, add the remaining oil through the
feeder tube. Set aside.

Reduce the oven temperature to 400°F/
200°C. Rinse the angler fish tail and pat it dry.
Wrap the ham around the angler fish and brush
lightly with oil. Season to taste with salt and

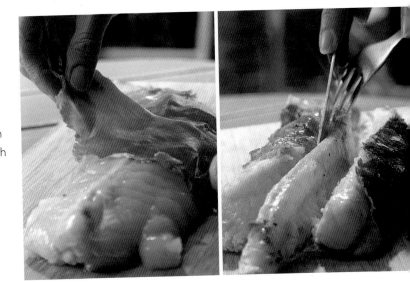

pepper. Place the fish on a baking sheet.

Roast the angler fish in the oven for
20 minutes until the flesh is opaque and flakes
easily. Test by lifting off the ham along the central
bone and cut a small amount of the flesh away
from the bone to see if it flakes.

Cut through the ham to remove the central
bone and produce 2 thick fillets. Cut each fillet
into 2 or 3 pieces and arrange on plates with a
spoonful of Romesco Sauce. Serve at once.

SERVE THIS WITH CHILI ROAST POTATOES OR
BOILED LONG-GRAIN RICE WITH CHOPPED FRESH
HERBS ADDED.

# GARLIC-CRUSTED
# ROAST HADDOCK

**SERVES 4**

2 lb/900 g mealy potatoes

1/2 cup milk

2 oz/55 g butter

4 haddock fillets, about
8 oz/225 g each

1 tbsp corn oil

4 garlic cloves,
finely chopped

salt and pepper

2 tbsp chopped fresh
parsley, to garnish

Preheat the oven to 450°F/230°C.

Cut the potatoes into chunks and cook in a pan of lightly salted water for 15 minutes, or until tender. Drain well. Mash in the pan until smooth. Set over low heat and beat in the milk, butter, and salt and pepper to taste.

Place the haddock fillets in a roasting pan and brush the fish with the oil. Sprinkle the garlic on top, add salt and pepper to taste, then spread with the mashed potatoes. Roast in the oven for 8–10 minutes, or until the fish is just tender.

Meanwhile, preheat the broiler. Transfer the fish to the broiler and cook for about 2 minutes, or until golden brown. Sprinkle with the chopped parsley and serve at once.

IF YOU PREFER, YOU CAN COOK THE POTATOES UNPEELED, BUT DO SCRUB THEM FIRST. PEEL THEM AS SOON AS THEY ARE COOL ENOUGH TO HANDLE, THEN MASH AS ABOVE. THIS HELPS TO PRESERVE THE VITAMINS AND MINERALS THAT LIE JUST BENEATH THE SKIN.

# ROAST PORGY
## WITH FENNEL

**SERVES 4**

2 cups dry, uncolored bread crumbs

2 tbsp milk

1 fennel bulb, thinly sliced, fronds reserved for garnishing

1 tbsp lemon juice

2 tbsp sambuca

1 tbsp chopped fresh thyme

1 dried bay leaf, crumbled

1 whole porgy, about 3 lb 5 oz/1.5 kg, cleaned, scaled, and boned

3 tbsp olive oil, plus extra for brushing

1 red onion, chopped

1¼ cups dry white wine

salt and pepper

lemon wedges, to serve

Preheat the oven to 475°F/240°C.

Place the bread crumbs in a bowl, add the milk, and set aside for 5 minutes to soak. Place the fennel in another bowl and add the lemon juice, sambuca, thyme, and bay leaf. Squeeze the bread crumbs and add them to the fennel mixture, stirring well.

Rinse the fish inside and out under cold running water and pat dry with paper towels. Season to taste with salt and pepper. Spoon the fennel mixture into the cavity, then bind the fish with trussing thread or kitchen string.

Brush a large ovenproof dish with oil and sprinkle the onion over the bottom. Lay the fish on top and pour in the wine—it should reach about one-third of the way up the fish. Drizzle the fish with the oil and roast in the oven for 25–30 minutes. Baste the fish occasionally with the cooking juices, and if it starts to brown, cover with a piece of foil to protect it.

Carefully lift out the porgy with a spatula, remove the string, and place on a warmed serving platter. Garnish with the reserved fennel fronds and serve at once with lemon wedges for squeezing over the fish.

SAMBUCA IS AN ITALIAN LIQUEUR DISTILLED FROM WITCH ELDER, BUT IT HAS A STRONG ANISE FLAVOR, WHICH MARRIES WELL WITH FISH. IF IT IS UNAVAILABLE, SUBSTITUTE PERNOD.

# ITALIAN COD

**SERVES 4**

2 tbsp butter

7/8 cup fresh whole wheat bread crumbs

1 heaping tbsp chopped walnuts

grated rind and juice of 2 lemons

2 fresh rosemary sprigs, stalks removed

2 tbsp chopped fresh parsley

4 cod fillets, about 5 1/2 oz/150 g each

1 garlic clove, crushed

1 small fresh red chili, diced

3 tbsp walnut oil

mixed salad greens, to serve

Preheat the oven to 400°F/200°C.

Melt the butter in a large pan over low heat, stirring constantly. Remove the pan from the heat and add the bread crumbs, walnuts, the rind and juice of 1 lemon, half the rosemary, and half the parsley, stirring until mixed.

Press the bread crumb mixture over the top of the cod fillets. Place the cod fillets in a shallow foil-lined roasting pan.

Roast the fish in the oven for 25–30 minutes.

Mix the garlic, the remaining lemon rind and juice, rosemary, parsley, and the chili together in a bowl. Beat in the oil and mix to combine. Drizzle the dressing over the cod steaks as soon as they are cooked.

Transfer the fish to warmed serving plates and serve at once with salad greens.

IF PREFERRED, THE WALNUTS MAY BE OMITTED FROM THE CRUST. IN ADDITION, EXTRA VIRGIN OLIVE OIL CAN BE USED INSTEAD OF WALNUT OIL, IF YOU LIKE.

# ROASTED MACKEREL
# MEDITERRANEAN-STYLE

**SERVES 4**

4 tbsp basil oil or extra
virgin olive oil

2 garlic cloves, chopped

1 onion, sliced

2 zucchini, sliced

6 plum tomatoes, sliced

12 black olives, pitted
and halved

1 tbsp tomato paste

4 tbsp red wine

generous 1/3 cup fish stock

2 tbsp chopped
fresh parsley

2 tbsp chopped fresh basil

4 large mackerel, cleaned

salt and pepper

*To garnish*

lemon slices

fresh basil sprigs

*To serve*

freshly cooked spaghetti

salad greens and scallions

Preheat the oven to 400°F/200°C.

Heat 1 tablespoon of the oil in a large skillet over medium heat. Add the garlic, onion, and zucchini and cook, stirring occasionally, for 4 minutes. Add the tomatoes, olives, tomato paste, wine, stock, herbs, and salt and pepper to taste. Bring to a boil, then reduce the heat to medium. Cook, stirring frequently, for 10 minutes.

Rinse the fish under cold running water, then pat dry with paper towels. Arrange the fish in a shallow ovenproof dish and drizzle the remaining oil over. Remove the skillet from the heat and spread the tomato sauce over the fish. Roast the fish in the center of the preheated oven for 10 minutes, or until they are cooked through.

Remove from the oven, arrange the fish in their sauce on plates of freshly cooked spaghetti, and garnish with lemon slices and sprigs of basil. Serve accompanied by a side salad of salad greens and scallions.

THE MEDITERRANEAN DIET IS SAID TO BE AMONG THE HEALTHIEST—THIS DISH IS A PERFECT EXAMPLE. MACKEREL PROVIDES ESSENTIAL FATTY ACIDS, OLIVE OIL IS HIGH IN VITAMIN A AND MONOUNSATURATED ("GOOD") FATS, WHILE TOMATOES, ESPECIALLY COOKED ONES, HAVE MANY HEALTH-ENHANCING PROPERTIES.

# FISH ROASTED WITH LIME

**SERVES 4**

2 lb 4 oz/1 kg white fish fillets, such as sea bass, flounder, or cod

1 lime, halved

3 tbsp extra virgin olive oil

1 large onion, finely chopped

3 garlic cloves, finely chopped

2–3 pickled jalapeño chilies (jalapeños en escabeche), chopped

6–8 tbsp chopped fresh cilantro

salt and pepper

lemon and lime wedges, to serve

Preheat the oven to 350°F/180°C.

Place the fish fillets in a nonmetallic bowl and season to taste with salt and pepper. Squeeze the juice from the lime halves over the fish.

Heat the oil in a skillet. Add the onion and garlic and cook, stirring frequently, for

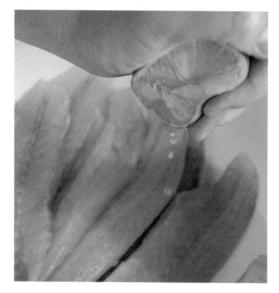

2 minutes, or until softened. Remove the skillet from the heat.

Place a third of the onion mixture and a little of the chilies and cilantro in the bottom of a shallow ovenproof dish or roasting pan. Arrange the fish on top. Top with the remaining onion mixture, chilies, and cilantro.

Roast in the oven for 15–20 minutes, or until the fish has become slightly opaque and firm to the touch. Serve at once, with lemon and lime wedges for squeezing over the fish.

TANGY AND SIMPLE TO PREPARE, THIS IS EXCELLENT SERVED WITH RICE AND BEANS FOR AN EASY LUNCH—SERVE WITH A GLASS OF CHILLED BEER.

No book about roasting food would be complete without roast potatoes, the perfect partner for roast meat and poultry. The many fans of this vegetable will be delighted to discover that there is more than one way to enjoy this superb accompaniment to a wide variety of dishes. Roast potatoes, served hot or cold, also make the most delicious snacks when sprinkled with salt and eaten with the fingers.

Other vegetables also lend themselves to this method of cooking. Roasting brings out the full flavor and a delightful sweetness in many root vegetables, such as carrots, parsnips, turnips, and sweet potatoes. Squashes, from butternuts to zucchini, and Mediterranean vegetables, such as tomatoes, eggplants, and bell peppers, make wonderful medleys that can be served as a vegetarian main course or as a side dish.

Still other vegetables, from onions to fennel, work well on their own. Roasting not only

# PART FOUR
# FRESH FROM THE GARDEN

develops a succulent depth of flavor, but often also creates an unusual crisp texture.

Serving roast vegetables, as a colorful mix or as individual high notes, with roast meat, poultry, game, or fish makes economic sense, too. If the oven will be switched on anyway, why not make full use of the space available? This helps save the housekeeping budget and uses fewer fuel resources. It also makes preparing a meal for family or guests almost trouble free, as roasting rarely requires a lot of attention and time in the kitchen. Mix and match the recipes from earlier chapters with those in this one, keeping an eye open for compatible oven temperatures and checking cooking times.

# PERFECT ROAST POTATOES

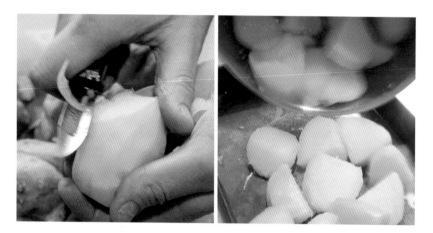

**SERVES 6**

3 lb/1.3 kg large potatoes,
such as round white,
round red, or fingerling,
peeled and cut into
even-size chunks

3 tbsp dripping, goose fat,
duck fat, or olive oil

salt

Preheat the oven to 425°F/220°C.

Cook the potatoes in a large pan of lightly salted boiling water over medium heat, covered, for 5–7 minutes. They will still be firm. Remove from the heat. Meanwhile, add the fat to a roasting pan and place in the hot oven.

Drain the potatoes well and return them to the pan. Cover with the lid and firmly shake the pan so that the surface of the potatoes is slightly roughened to help give them a much crisper texture.

Remove the roasting pan from the oven and carefully tip the potatoes into the hot fat. Baste them to ensure that they are all coated with it.

Roast the potatoes at the top of the oven for 45–50 minutes until they are browned all over and thoroughly crisp. Turn the potatoes and baste again only once during the process or the crunchy edges will be destroyed.

Using a slotted spoon, carefully transfer the potatoes from the roasting pan into a warmed serving dish. Sprinkle with a little salt and serve at once. Any leftovers (although this is most unlikely) are delicious cold.

PERFECT ROAST POTATOES ARE CRISP ON THE OUTSIDE AND SOFT AND FLUFFY ON THE INSIDE. DO CHOOSE THE RIGHT POTATOES—MEALY ONES ARE BEST. THE CHOICE OF FAT IS ALSO IMPORTANT— GOOSE OR DUCK FAT GIVES AN AMAZING FLAVOR. HOWEVER, THE FAT FROM A JOINT IS ALMOST AS GOOD AND REALLY TASTY POTATOES CAN ALSO BE MADE USING OLIVE OIL. PARBOILING THE POTATOES IS A CHORE BUT WORTHWHILE BECAUSE IT GIVES CRUSTY OUTSIDES. HOWEVER, IF YOU PREFER NOT TO DO IT, SUBSTITUTE SMALL, WHOLE, UNPEELED NEW POTATOES, WHICH DO NOT NEED PARBOILING. SIMPLY COAT THEM IN THE HOT FAT AND ROAST FOR 30–40 MINUTES. IN BOTH CASES, A HEAVY ROASTING PAN WILL ENSURE THAT THE POTATOES DON'T STICK, AND A HOT OVEN MEANS THAT THEY CRISP, NOT STEAM, IN THE FAT.

# ROASTED GARLIC
# MASHED POTATOES

**SERVES 4**

2 whole garlic bulbs

1 tbsp olive oil

2 lb/900 g mealy
potatoes, peeled

1/2 cup milk

2 oz/55 g butter

salt and pepper

Preheat the oven to 350°F/180°C.

Separate the garlic cloves, place on a large piece of foil, and drizzle with the oil. Wrap the garlic in the foil and roast in the oven for about 1 hour, or until very tender. Let cool slightly.

Twenty minutes before the end of the cooking time, cut the potatoes into chunks, then cook in a pan of lightly salted boiling water for 15 minutes, or until tender.

Meanwhile, squeeze the cooled garlic cloves out of their skins and push through a strainer into a pan. Add the milk, butter, and salt and pepper to taste and heat gently until the butter has melted.

Drain the cooked potatoes, then mash in the pan until smooth. Pour in the garlic mixture and heat gently, stirring, until the ingredients are combined. Serve hot.

WHEN ROASTED, GARLIC LOSES ITS PUNGENT ACIDITY AND ACQUIRES A DELICIOUS, FULL-FLAVORED SWEETNESS. SO ALTHOUGH USING TWO WHOLE BULBS MAY SEEM EXCESSIVE, YOU WILL BE SURPRISED AT THE UNIQUELY MELLOW FLAVOR. IN ADDITION, ROASTED GARLIC LEAVES VERY LITTLE TRACE OF ITS SMELL ON THE BREATH.

# CHILI ROAST POTATOES

**SERVES 4**

1 lb 2 oz/500 g small new potatoes, scrubbed

2/3 cup vegetable oil

1 tsp chili powder

1/2 tsp caraway seeds

1 tsp salt

Preheat the oven to 400°F/200°C. Cook the potatoes in a large pan of boiling water for 10 minutes, then drain thoroughly.

Meanwhile, pour a little of the oil into a shallow roasting pan to coat the bottom. Heat the oil in the oven for 10 minutes, then remove the pan from the oven. Add the potatoes and brush them with the hot oil.

Mix the chili powder, caraway seeds, and salt together in a small bowl, then sprinkle the mixture evenly over the potatoes, turning them to coat. Add the remaining oil to the pan and return to the oven to roast for 15 minutes, or until the potatoes are cooked through and golden brown.

Using a slotted spoon, remove the potatoes from the pan, drain well, transfer to a large warmed serving dish, and serve at once.

FOR THIS DELICIOUS SIDE DISH, SMALL NEW POTATOES ARE SCRUBBED AND BOILED IN THEIR SKINS, BEFORE BEING COATED IN A HOT CHILI MIXTURE AND ROASTED TO PERFECTION IN THE OVEN.

# ROASTED ROOT VEGETABLES

**SERVES 4–6**

3 parsnips, cut into
2-inch/5-cm chunks

4 baby turnips, quartered

3 carrots, cut into
2-inch/5-cm chunks

1 lb/450 g butternut
squash, peeled and cut
into 2-inch/5-cm chunks

1 lb/450 g sweet potatoes,
peeled and cut into
2-inch/5-cm chunks

2 garlic cloves,
finely chopped

2 tbsp chopped
fresh rosemary

2 tbsp chopped
fresh thyme

2 tsp chopped fresh sage

3 tbsp olive oil

salt and pepper

2 tbsp chopped fresh
mixed herbs, such as
parsley, thyme, and mint,
to garnish

Preheat the oven to 425°F/220°C.

Arrange all the vegetables in a single layer in
a large roasting pan. Sprinkle over the garlic and
the herbs. Pour over the oil and season well with
salt and pepper.

Toss all the ingredients together until they
are well mixed and coated with the oil (you can
let them marinate at this stage to allow the
flavors to be absorbed).

Roast the vegetables at the top of the oven
for 50–60 minutes until they are cooked and
nicely browned. Turn the vegetables over
halfway through the cooking time.

Serve with a good handful of fresh herbs
sprinkled on top and a final seasoning of salt and
pepper to taste.

ROASTED ROOT VEGETABLES ARE PARTICULARLY POPULAR SINCE THEY ALL COOK TOGETHER
AND NEED LITTLE ATTENTION ONCE PREPARED. YOU CAN USE WHATEVER IS AVAILABLE:
POTATOES, PARSNIPS, TURNIPS, RUTABAGAS, CARROTS, AND, ALTHOUGH NOT STRICTLY
ROOT VEGETABLES, SQUASH AND ONIONS. SHALLOTS OR WEDGES OF RED ONION ADD
EXTRA COLOR, FLAVOR, AND TEXTURE, AND WHOLE, UNPEELED GARLIC CLOVES ARE ALSO
A TASTY ADDITION. TRY TO HAVE ALL THE VEGETABLES CUT TO ROUGHLY THE SAME SIZE.
IT'S ALWAYS A GOOD IDEA TO USE A GENEROUS HANDFUL OF HERBS, PARTICULARLY A
MIXTURE OF THE STRONGER-FLAVORED AND MOST AROMATIC ONES, SUCH AS ROSEMARY,
THYME, AND SAGE.

# ROAST SUMMER VEGETABLES

**SERVES 4**

2 tbsp olive oil

1 fennel bulb

2 red onions

2 beefsteak tomatoes

1 eggplant

2 zucchini

1 yellow bell pepper

1 red bell pepper

1 orange bell pepper

4 garlic cloves, peeled but left whole

4 fresh rosemary sprigs

pepper

crusty bread, to serve (optional)

Preheat the oven to 400°F/200°C.

Brush a large ovenproof dish with a little of the oil. Prepare the vegetables. Cut the fennel bulb, red onions, and tomatoes into wedges. Slice the eggplant and zucchini thickly, then seed all the bell peppers and cut into chunks. Arrange the vegetables in the dish and tuck the garlic cloves and rosemary sprigs among them. Drizzle with the remaining oil and season to taste with pepper.

Roast the vegetables in the oven for 10 minutes. Remove the dish from the oven and turn the vegetables over using a slotted spoon. Return the dish to the oven and roast for an additional 10–15 minutes, or until the vegetables are tender and starting to turn golden brown.

Serve the vegetables straight from the dish or transfer them to a warmed serving plate. For a vegetarian main course, serve with crusty bread, if you like.

THIS APPETIZING AND COLORFUL MIXTURE OF MEDITERRANEAN VEGETABLES MAKES A SENSATIONAL SUMMER LUNCH FOR VEGETARIANS AND MEAT-EATERS ALIKE. ROASTING BRINGS OUT THE FULL FLAVOR AND SWEETNESS OF THE BELL PEPPERS, EGGPLANTS, ZUCCHINI, AND ONIONS.

# ROASTED ONIONS

**SERVES 4**

8 large onions, peeled but
left whole

3 tbsp olive oil

2 oz/55 g butter

2 tsp chopped
fresh thyme

7 oz/200 g Cheddar or
Lancashire cheese, grated

salt and pepper

*To serve*

salad

warm crusty bread

Preheat the oven to 350°F/180°C.

Cut a cross down through the top of each onion toward the root, without cutting all the way through. Place the onions in a roasting pan and drizzle over the oil.

Press a little of the butter into the open crosses, sprinkle with the thyme, and season to taste with salt and pepper. Cover with foil and roast in the oven for 40–45 minutes.

Remove the pan from the oven, take off and discard the foil, and baste the onions with the pan juices. Return to the oven and cook for an additional 15 minutes, uncovered, to let the onions brown.

Take the onions out of the oven and sprinkle the grated cheese over them. Return them to the oven for a few minutes so that the cheese starts to melt.

Serve at once with some salad and lots of warm crusty bread.

FOR DRESSED ONIONS, BOIL 4 PEELED ONIONS IN SALTED WATER FOR 20 MINUTES. SCOOP OUT THE CENTERS WITH A TEASPOON AND FILL WITH A MIXTURE OF $^{1}/_{2}$ CUP GRATED CHEESE, 1 CUP FRESH BREAD CRUMBS, AND 1 TEASPOON MUSTARD. PLACE THE ONIONS IN AN OVENPROOF DISH, DOT WITH 2 TABLESPOONS BUTTER, AND ROAST IN A PREHEATED OVEN, 425°F/220°C, FOR 25–30 MINUTES. SERVE HOT AS AN APPETIZER OR AS AN ACCOMPANIMENT TO ROAST MEAT.

# OVEN-DRIED TOMATOES

**MAKES 1 × 1/2-PINT/ 250 ML JAR**

2 lb 4 oz/1 kg large, juicy, full-flavored tomatoes

extra virgin olive oil

sea salt

Preheat the oven to 250°F/120°C.

Using a sharp knife, cut each of the tomatoes into quarters.

Using a teaspoon, scoop out the seeds and discard. If the tomatoes are large, cut each quarter in half lengthwise again.

Sprinkle sea salt in a roasting pan and arrange the tomato slices, skin-side down, on top. Roast in the oven for 2 1/2 hours, or until the edges are just starting to look charred and the flesh is dry, but still pliable. The exact roasting time and yield will depend on the size and juiciness of the tomatoes. Check the tomatoes at 30-minute intervals after 1 1/2 hours.

Remove the dried tomatoes from the roasting pan and let cool completely. Place in a 1/2-pint preserving jar and pour over enough oil to cover. Seal the jar tightly and store in the refrigerator, where the tomatoes will keep for up to 2 weeks.

SERVE THESE OVEN-DRIED TOMATOES WITH SLICES OF BUFFALO MOZZARELLA—DRIZZLE WITH OLIVE OIL AND SPRINKLE WITH COARSELY GROUND PEPPER AND FINELY TORN BASIL LEAVES.

# CRISPY ROAST ASPARAGUS

**SERVES 4**

1 lb/450 g asparagus spears

2 tbsp extra virgin olive oil

1 tsp coarse sea salt

1 tbsp freshly grated Parmesan cheese, to serve

Preheat the oven to 400°F/200°C.

Choose asparagus spears of similar widths. Trim the base of the spears so that all the stems are approximately the same length.

Arrange the asparagus in a single layer on a baking sheet. Drizzle with the oil and sprinkle with the salt.

Place the baking sheet in the oven and roast the asparagus for 10–15 minutes, turning the spears once. Remove from the oven and transfer to a warmed dish. Serve at once, sprinkled with Parmesan cheese.

AS WELL AS THERE BEING BOTH GREEN AND WHITE VARIETIES, ASPARAGUS VARIES CONSIDERABLY IN WIDTH, SO IT IS IMPORTANT TO TRY TO FIND SPEARS OF A SIMILAR SIZE. OTHERWISE, SOME WILL BE TENDER WHILE OTHERS REQUIRE FURTHER COOKING. AS A GENERAL RULE, THE STEMS OF GREEN ASPARAGUS RARELY NEED PEELING, BUT THOSE OF WHITE ASPARAGUS DO.

# CRISPY ROASTED FENNEL

**SERVES 4–6**

3 large fennel bulbs

4 tbsp olive oil

juice and finely grated rind of 1 small lemon

1 garlic clove, finely chopped

1 cup fresh white bread crumbs

salt and pepper

Preheat the oven to 400°F/200°C.

Trim the fennel bulbs, reserving the green feathery fronds, and cut into quarters. Cook the bulbs in a large pan of boiling salted water for 5 minutes until just tender, then drain well.

Heat half the oil in a small roasting pan or ovenproof dish, add the fennel, and turn to coat in the oil. Drizzle over the lemon juice.

Roast the fennel in the oven for 35 minutes, or until starting to brown.

Meanwhile, heat the remaining oil in a skillet. Add the garlic and sauté for 1 minute until lightly browned. Add the bread crumbs and sauté, stirring frequently, for 5 minutes, or until crispy. Remove from the heat and stir in the lemon rind, reserved snipped fennel fronds, and salt and pepper to taste.

When the fennel is cooked, sprinkle the bread crumb mixture over the top, and return to the oven for an additional 5 minutes. Serve hot.

IT IS SAID THAT MALE FENNEL HAS MORE FLAVOR THAN FEMALE FENNEL. TO DISTINGUISH ONE FROM THE OTHER, THE MALE IS LONG AND THIN, WHILE THE FEMALE IS ROUNDED AND BULBOUS.

# ROAST LEEKS

**SERVES 6**

4 leeks

3 tbsp olive oil

2 tsp balsamic vinegar

sea salt and pepper

IF IN SEASON, 8 BABY LEEKS MAY BE USED INSTEAD OF THE STANDARD-SIZED ONES. SHERRY VINEGAR MAKES A GOOD SUBSTITUTE FOR THE EXPENSIVE BALSAMIC VINEGAR AND WOULD WORK AS WELL IN THIS RECIPE.

Preheat the oven to 400°F/200°C.

Halve the leeks lengthwise, making sure that your knife cuts straight, so that the leek is held together by the root. Rinse thoroughly, fanning the layers gently, under cold running water to remove all traces of soil and grit. Pat dry with paper towels.

Place the leeks in a single layer in a roasting pan and brush with the oil. Roast in the oven for 20–30 minutes until tender and just starting to color.

Remove the leeks from the oven and brush with balsamic vinegar. Sprinkle with salt and pepper to taste and serve hot or warm.

# INDEX